JAMES

JAMES

Published in Dallas by Love God Greatly.

Special thanks to:
Contributing Photographer: Meshali Mitchell
Contributing Recipe: Gloria Martucci

Printed in the United States of America

Library of Congress Cataloging-in-Publication Data

Printed in the United States of America

22 21 20 19 18 17

6 5 4 3 2 1

AT LOVE GOD GREATLY, YOU'LL FIND
REAL, AUTHENTIC WOMEN. WOMEN WHO
ARE IMPERFECT, YET FORGIVEN.

Women who desire less of us, and a whole lot
more of Jesus. Women who long to know God
through his Word, because we know that Truth
transforms and sets us free. Women who are
better together, saturated in God's Word and in
community with one another.

Welcome, friend. We're so glad you're here...

CONTENTS

WELCOME

We are glad you have decided to join us in this Bible study! First of all, please know that you have been prayed for! It is not a coincidence you are participating in this study.

Our prayer for you is simple: that you will grow closer to our Lord as you dig into His Word each and every day! As you develop the discipline of being in God's Word on a daily basis, our prayer is that you will fall in love with Him even more as you spend time reading from the Bible.

Each day before you read the assigned Scripture(s), pray and ask God to help you understand it. Invite Him to speak to you through His Word. Then listen. It's His job to speak to you, and it's your job to listen and obey.

As you go through this study, join us in the following resources below:

Take time to read the verses over and over again. We are told in Proverbs to search and you will find: "Search for it like silver, and hunt for it like hidden treasure. Then you will understand" (Prov. 2:4–5 NCV).

Weekly Blog Posts •

Weekly Memory Verses •

Weekly Challenges •

Facebook, Twitter, Instagram •

LoveGodGreatly.com •

Hashtags: #LoveGodGreatly •

All of us here at Love God Greatly can't wait for you to get started, and we hope to see you at the finish line. Endure, persevere, press on—and don't give up! Finish well what you are beginning today. We will be here every step of the way, cheering you on! We are in this together. Fight to rise early, to push back the stress of the day, to sit alone and spend time in God's Word! Let's see what God has in store for you in this study! Journey with us as we learn to love God greatly with our lives!

RESOURCES

Join Us

ONLINE

lovegodgreatly.com

STORE

lovegodgreatly.com/store

FACEBOOK

facebook.com/LoveGodGreatly

INSTAGRAM

instagram.com/lovegodgreatlyofficial

TWITTER

@_LoveGodGreatly

DOWNLOAD THE APP

CONTACT US

info@lovegodgreatly.com

CONNECT

#LoveGodGreatly

LOVE
GOD
GREATLY

Love God Greatly (LGG) is a beautiful community of women who use a variety of technology platforms to keep each other accountable in God's Word. We start with a simple Bible reading plan, but it doesn't stop there.

Some women gather in homes and churches locally, while others connect online with women across the globe. Whatever the method, we lovingly lock arms and unite for this purpose: to love God greatly with our lives.

Would you consider reaching out and doing this study with someone?

In today's fast-paced technology-driven world, it would be easy to study God's Word in an isolated environment that lacks encouragement or support, but that isn't the intention here at Love God Greatly. God created us to live in community with Him and with those around us.

We need each other, and we live life better together. Because of this, would you consider reaching out and doing this study with someone?

Rest assured we'll be studying right alongside you—learning with you, cheering for you, enjoying sweet fellowship, and smiling from ear to ear as we watch God unite women together—intentionally connecting hearts and minds for His glory.

So here's the challenge: call your mom, your sister, your grandma, the girl across the street, or the college friend across the country. Gather a group of girls from your church or workplace, or meet in a coffee shop with friends you have always wished you knew better.

Arm-in-arm and hand-in-hand, let's do this thing...together.

SOAP STUDY
HOW AND WHY TO SOAP

In this study we offer you a study journal to accompany the verses we are reading. This journal is designed to help you interact with God's Word and learn to dig deeper, encouraging you to slow down and reflect on what God is saying to you that day.

At Love God Greatly, we use the SOAP Bible study method. Before beginning, let's take a moment to define this method and share why we recommend using it during your quiet time in the following pages.

It's one thing to simply read Scripture. But when you interact with it, intentionally slowing down to really reflect on it, suddenly words start popping off the page. The SOAP method allows you to dig deeper into Scripture and see more than you would if you simply read the verses and then went on your merry way.

The most important ingredients in the Soap method are your interaction with God's Word and your application of His Word to your life.

The most important ingredients in the SOAP method are your interaction with God's Word and your application of His Word to your life:

Blessed is the one who does not walk in step with the wicked or stand in the way that sinners take or sit in the company of mockers, but whose delight is in the law of the LORD, and who meditates on his law day and night. That person is like a tree planted by streams of water, which yields its fruit in season and whose leaf does not wither—whatever they do prospers. (Ps. 1:1–3, NIV)

Please take the time to SOAP through our Bible studies and see for yourself how much more you get from your daily reading.

You'll be amazed.

SOAP STUDY *(CONTINUED)*
WHAT DOES SOAP MEAN?

S STANDS FOR
SCRIPTURE

Physically write out the verses.

You'll be amazed at what God will reveal to you just by taking the time to slow down and write out what you are reading!

MONDAY

READ
Colossians 1:5–8

SOAP
Colossians 1:5–8

Scripture

WRITE
OUT THE
SCRIPTURE
PASSAGE
FOR THE
DAY.

The faith and love that spring from the hope stored up for you in heaven and about which you have already heard in the true message of the gospel that has come to you. In the same way, the gospel is bearing fruit and growing throughout the whole world just as it has been doing among you since the day you heard it and truly understood God's grace. You learned it from Epaphras, our dear fellow servant, who is a faithful minister of Christ on our behalf, and who also told us of your love in the Spirit.

Observations

WRITE
DOWN 1 OR 2
OBSERVATIONS
FROM THE
PASSAGE

When you combine faith and love, you get hope. We must remember that our hope is in heaven, it is yet to come. The gospel is the Word of truth. The gospel is continually bearing fruit and growing from the first day to the last. It just takes one person to change a whole community, Epaphras.

O STANDS FOR
OBSERVATION

What do you see in the verses that you're reading?

Who is the intended audience? Is there a repetition of words?

What words stand out to you?

A STANDS FOR **APPLICATION**

This is when God's Word becomes personal.

What is God saying to you today?

How can you apply what you just read to your own personal life?

What changes do you need to make? Is there action you need to take?

Applications

WRITE DOWN 1 OR 2 APPLICATIONS FROM THE PASSAGE.

God used one man, Epaphras, to change a whole town. I was reminded that we are simply called to tell others about Christ; it's God's job to spread the gospel, to grow it, and have it bear fruit. I felt today a verses were almost directly spoken to Love God Greatly women: "The gospel is bearing fruit and growing throughout the whole world just as it has been doing among you since the day you heard it and truly understood God's grace.

Pray

WRITE OUT A PRAYER OVER WHAT YOU LEARNED FROM TODAY'S PASSAGE.

Dear Lord, please help me to be an Epaphras, to tell others about You and then leave the results in Your loving hands. Please help me to understand and apply personally what I have read today to my life, thereby becoming more and more like You each and every day. Help me to live a life that bears the fruit of faith and love, anchoring my hope in heaven, not here on earth. Help me to remember that the best is yet to come!

P STANDS FOR **PRAYER**

Pray God's Word back to Him. Spend time thanking Him.

If He has revealed something to you during this time in His Word, pray about it.

If He has revealed some sin that is in your life, confess. And remember, He loves you dearly.

A RECIPE FOR YOU

TIRAMISÙ

Ingredients

6 eggs, separated

150 g (3/4 cup) sugar

500 g (2 ¼ cups) mascarpone

300 g (10.5 oz) savoiardi biscuits

750 ml (3 cups) espresso

Cocoa powder

Directions

- Prepare the espresso and set aside to cool.

- Add the sugar to the egg yolks. Beat well until the mixture is light and creamy.

- Add the sugar and yolk mixture to mascarpone a little bit at a time and mix until combined.

- In a separate bowl, beat the egg whites until stiff. Gently fold the beaten egg whites into the mascarpone mixture.

- Pour espresso into a shallow dish. Quickly dip each savoiardi biscuit in the espresso, dipping one at a time just long enough to wet biscuits (do not soak them!). Line the bottom of a 20 cm (8 in.) square glass dish with the dipped biscuits.

- Once the biscuits cover the bottom of the dish, spoon half of the mascarpone mixture over the top of the biscuits. Dust with cocoa. Repeat process with another savoiardi biscuit layer, then the remaining mascarpone, and a final dusting of cocoa powder.

- Chill in refrigerator for about 4 hours, then enjoy!

LGG ITALIAN TESTIMONY

GLORIA, ITALY

Hello, I'm Gloria and I am 31 years old. I was born into a Christian family in Italy and I invited Jesus into my heart when I was nine years old. I grew up with a lot of doubts and dissatisfaction until God spoke to my heart through the loss of my 20 year-old cousin to cancer. After this I decided to not complain anymore for the things God had not given to me, but rather to thank Him for all He has given to me by His grace.

There was a community ready to pray for me.

I got married to a man from Guatemala and together we served in our church with children, youth, and women's ministries until two years ago. God brought the ministry of *Love God Greatly* into my life in a season when I was so discouraged because I felt useless and alone. Through *Love God Greatly* God showed me that I was not alone because there was a community ready to pray for me, and that I could be helpful by translating Bible studies for the women in my country and abroad.

Since I started translating the studies I found that God was blessing me at least three times during the translation process because I need to read the blogs and devotionals at least three times before sharing them. So, God repeats His sweet words to me several times each study! I love being a part of the *Love God Greatly* community as a translator and facilitator because it's a wonderful opportunity to make available these great resources to Italian women and lead them deeper into God's Word.

Love God Greatly is very important in my language because it offers a method to study the Bible that is not so developed in Italy. We, as Europeans, are used to meditating on the Bible through devotionals written by other people – this is seen as easier, more comfortable and, above all, it's faster. But *Love God Greatly's* SOAP method offers an introspective method. You have to write down YOUR impressions, YOUR feelings, and what God is speaking to YOU in that moment. It's also helpful in a small group because it offers an opportunity to discuss what we are learning with other women... a perfect fit since Italians are famous for speaking, eating, and enjoying community!

LGG ITALIAN TESTIMONY

VALERIA, GERMANY

My name is Valeria Elisabetta Milillo, and I'm 33 years old. I live in Germany but I come from Italy. Six years ago I surrendered my life to Jesus. After my conversion, the Lord blessed me with the children I had so longed for.

With the birth of my second daughter, however, it was difficult for me to attend church and join a Christian community because my church was in a different country than where I lived. That was when I found *Love God Greatly* and began studying God's Word. I was really in love with the studies, so I started to translate them and post them in a Facebook group specifically created for *Love God Greatly* in Italian. I contacted Angela Perritt to formalize this project and slowly the group began to grow. In 2015 Gloria joined me as a translator.

In these years *Love God Greatly* has strengthened my walk with God. God has used His Word to speak to me, comfort me, and lead me. Very often a blog post or a verse has been the right encouragement at just the right time.

I moved to Germany in 2015. The nearest church is very far – one and a half hours from my house. Because I have no driver's license and my husband works, I cannot attend the church. This situation still hurts me, but *Love God Greatly* is a great blessing and is the lifesaver that the Lord brought to me as I wait for His plans for me and my family.

To connect with LGG Italian Branch:

- https://www.facebook.com/
  LoveGodGreatlyITALIA/
- lovegodgreatlyitalia@hotmail.com

Do you know someone who could use our *Love God Greatly* Bible studies in Italian? If so, make sure and tell them about LGG Italia and all the amazing Bible study resources we provide to help equip them with God's Word!!!

In these years Love God Greatly has strengthened my walk with God. God has used His Word to speak to me, comfort me, and lead me.

JAMES

Let's Begin

INTRODUCTION

JAMES

When you read the book of James in the New Testament, you're reading something that was written by the half-brother of Jesus. How amazing to be able to read words written by a man who grew up in the same home as our Lord.

James is never listed as one of the followers of Jesus during His earthly ministry. In fact, we don't really know much about him until his adult years. This is probably because James did not become a believer until after Christ's resurrection (John 7:3-5; Acts 1:14).

So what do we know about James, the brother of Jesus? He held a high and important leadership role in the church (Galatians 2:9) and from church history we know that he was a part of the first ecumenical council of the early church that was called in order to address some of the early heresies. The presiding officer was James, not Peter or Paul.

James was known for being a just man and one who loved righteousness. Tradition says that his knees resembled the knees of camels because he spent a lot of his life on his knees in prayer. So his nickname became James the Just, or James the Righteous.

Sometime around 50 AD the Spirit inspired this brother of Jesus to write a book. Since James and Jesus came from the same family you'd almost expect his book to be written like one of the Gospels, in which he tells stories about his divine brother. But never once does he say, "and Jesus said ..." or "Jesus did..." Instead, his writing style is more like the wisdom literature that is found in the book of Proverbs.

R.C. Sproul points out that James writes similarly to the way that Jesus taught, not in long lectures, but in short lessons. The book of James is not very long, but James does manage to teach on a number of different topics. Like Jesus, he talks to us about suffering, the power of prayer, the importance of controlling our tongue, and the danger of wealth.

When we compare the writings of Paul to those of James, we see that Paul's writings, though practical, focus more on "orthodoxy" (right thinking). James, on the other hand, was more focused on "orthopraxy" (right living). His focus was on our hearts and hands more than on our hearts and minds. But don't misunderstand James; both theology and godliness are important to a robust Christian life. In fact, you can't live rightly if you don't first think rightly. The right doctrine, received by faith, leads to proper devotion.

Because James' emphasis is on what we do, many have misunderstood the book. Some read it in such a way that they believe we can earn or maintain God's love and favor through our works. This is a heresy that can lead people away from the gospel. Believers who begin to read James like this will run into two potential problems: despair or pride. If you believe that God accepts you based on your behavior you might despair and quickly give up when you fail (and we all fail often). If you don't despair over your failure, you will struggle with pride when you succeed.

The proper way to read James is through the lens of the gospel. Without that, the entire text will be out of focus. James is a picture of the perfect Christian life. But no one is perfect, not even one (Romans 3:23). Therefore, instead of feeling despair when we fail, we need to look to Jesus who lived that perfect life for us, and rejoice that in Him all our sins are forgiven. And instead of being prideful when we succeed, we need to be thankful that Christ is at work in us.

James challenges us to not only talk the talk, but walk the walk. As we study through this book together, may we be confronted with our shortcomings and repent, encouraged by Christ's abundant grace, and motivated to live godly lives through His power and for His glory.

READING PLAN

WEEK 1

Monday
READ: JAMES 1:1-4
SOAP: JAMES 1:1-4

Tuesday
READ: JAMES 1:5-8
SOAP: JAMES 1:5-8

Wednesday
READ: JAMES 1:9-11
SOAP: JAMES 1:9-11

Thursday
READ: JAMES 1:12-15
SOAP: JAMES 1:12-15

Friday
READ: JAMES 1:16-18
SOAP: JAMES 1:16-18

WEEK 2

Monday
READ: JAMES 1:19-21
SOAP: JAMES 1:19-21

Tuesday
READ: JAMES 1:22-27
SOAP: JAMES 1:22-27

Wednesday
READ: JAMES 2:1-7
SOAP: JAMES 2:1-7

Thursday
READ: JAMES 2:8-13
SOAP: JAMES 2:8-9

Friday
READ: JAMES 2:14-26
SOAP: JAMES 2:14-17

WEEK 3

Monday
READ: JAMES 3:1-5
SOAP: JAMES 3:3-5

Tuesday
READ: JAMES 3:6-12
SOAP: JAMES 3:8-10

Wednesday
READ: JAMES 3:13-18
SOAP: JAMES 3:17-18

Thursday
READ: JAMES 4:1-6
SOAP: JAMES 4:4-6

Friday
READ: JAMES 4:7-12
SOAP: JAMES 4:7-8

WEEK 4

Monday
READ: JAMES 4:13-17
SOAP: JAMES 4:13-17

Tuesday
READ: JAMES 5:1-6
SOAP: JAMES 5:1-3

Wednesday
READ: JAMES 5:7-12
SOAP: JAMES 5:7-8

Thursday
READ: JAMES 5:13-18
SOAP: JAMES 5:13-16

Friday
READ: JAMES 5:19-20
SOAP: JAMES 5:19-20

YOUR
GOALS

We believe it's important to write out goals for this study. Take some time now and write three goals you would like to focus on as you begin to rise each day and dig into God's Word. Make sure and refer back to these goals throughout the next weeks to help you stay focused. You can do it!

1.

2.

3.

Signature:

Date:

WEEK 1

Count it all joy, my brothers, when you meet trials of various kinds, for you know that the testing of your faith produces steadfastness.

JAMES 1:2-3

PRAYER

WRITE DOWN YOUR PRAYER REQUESTS
AND PRAISES FOR EACH DAY.

Prayer focus for this week:
Spend time praying for your family members.

MONDAY

TUESDAY

WEDNESDAY

THURSDAY

FRIDAY

CHALLENGE

You can find this listed in our Monday blog post.

MONDAY
Scripture for Week 1

James 1:1-4

1 James, a servant of God and of the Lord Jesus Christ,
To the twelve tribes in the Dispersion:
Greetings.

2 Count it all joy, my brothers, when you meet trials of various kinds, 3 for you know that the testing of your faith produces steadfastness. 4 And let steadfastness have its full effect, that you may be perfect and complete, lacking in nothing.

MONDAY

READ:
James 1:1-4

SOAP:
James 1:1-4

Scripture

WRITE
OUT THE
SCRIPTURE
PASSAGE
FOR THE
DAY.

1 James a servant of God &
the Lord Jesus Christ to the 12
tribes in the dispersion

Count it all joy my brothers when
you meet trials of various kinds
for you know that the testing of your
faith produces steadfastness And
let steadfastness have its perfect
work (full effect)

Observations

WRITE
DOWN 1 OR 2
OBSERVATIONS
FROM THE
PASSAGE.

Applications

WRITE
DOWN 1 OR 2
APPLICATIONS
FROM THE
PASSAGE.

Pray

WRITE OUT
A PRAYER
OVER WHAT
YOU LEARNED
FROM TODAY'S
PASSAGE.

TUESDAY
Scripture for Week 1

James 1:5-8

5 If any of you lacks wisdom, let him ask God, who gives generously to all without reproach, and it will be given him. 6 But let him ask in faith, with no doubting, for the one who doubts is like a wave of the sea that is driven and tossed by the wind. 7 For that person must not suppose that he will receive anything from the Lord; 8 he is a double-minded man, unstable in all his ways.

TUESDAY

READ:
James 1:5-8

SOAP:
James 1:5-8

Scripture

WRITE
OUT THE
SCRIPTURE
PASSAGE
FOR THE
DAY.

Observations

WRITE
DOWN 1 OR 2
OBSERVATIONS
FROM THE
PASSAGE.

Applications

WRITE
DOWN 1 OR 2
APPLICATIONS
FROM THE
PASSAGE.

Pray

WRITE OUT
A PRAYER
OVER WHAT
YOU LEARNED
FROM TODAY'S
PASSAGE.

WEDNESDAY
Scripture for Week 1

James 1:9-11

9 Let the lowly brother boast in his exaltation, 10 and the rich in his humiliation, because like a flower of the grass he will pass away. 11 For the sun rises with its scorching heat and withers the grass; its flower falls, and its beauty perishes. So also will the rich man fade away in the midst of his pursuits.

WEDNESDAY

READ:
James 1:9-11

SOAP:
James 1:9-11

Scripture

WRITE
OUT THE
SCRIPTURE
PASSAGE
FOR THE
DAY.

Observations

WRITE
DOWN 1 OR 2
OBSERVATIONS
FROM THE
PASSAGE.

Applications

WRITE
DOWN 1 OR 2
APPLICATIONS
FROM THE
PASSAGE.

Pray

WRITE OUT
A PRAYER
OVER WHAT
YOU LEARNED
FROM TODAY'S
PASSAGE.

THURSDAY

Scripture for Week 1

James 1:12-15

12 Blessed is the man who remains steadfast under trial, for when he has stood the test he will receive the crown of life, which God has promised to those who love him. 13 Let no one say when he is tempted, "I am being tempted by God," for God cannot be tempted with evil, and he himself tempts no one. 14 But each person is tempted when he is lured and enticed by his own desire. 15 Then desire when it has conceived gives birth to sin, and sin when it is fully grown brings forth death.

THURSDAY

READ:
James 1:12-15

SOAP:
James 1:12-15

Scripture

WRITE
OUT THE
SCRIPTURE
PASSAGE
FOR THE
DAY.

Observations

WRITE
DOWN 1 OR 2
OBSERVATIONS
FROM THE
PASSAGE.

Applications

WRITE
DOWN 1 OR 2
APPLICATIONS
FROM THE
PASSAGE.

Pray

WRITE OUT
A PRAYER
OVER WHAT
YOU LEARNED
FROM TODAY'S
PASSAGE.

FRIDAY
Scripture for Week 1

James 1:16-18

16 Do not be deceived, my beloved brothers. 17 Every
good gift and every perfect gift is from above, coming down
from the Father of lights, with whom there is no variation
or shadow due to change. 18 Of his own will he brought
us forth by the word of truth, that we should be a kind
of firstfruits of his creatures.

FRIDAY

READ:
James 1:16-18

SOAP:
James 1:16-18

Scripture

WRITE
OUT THE
SCRIPTURE
PASSAGE
FOR THE
DAY.

Observations

WRITE
DOWN 1 OR 2
OBSERVATIONS
FROM THE
PASSAGE.

Applications

WRITE
DOWN 1 OR 2
APPLICATIONS
FROM THE
PASSAGE.

Pray

WRITE OUT
A PRAYER
OVER WHAT
YOU LEARNED
FROM TODAY'S
PASSAGE.

REFLECTION QUESTIONS

1. What should trials produce in the life of a Christian? Why should we be joyful in the midst of trials?

2. Why is it important to pray with faith? How is the person who doubts "unstable in all his ways"?

3. What is the warning to the rich? Why do they need this warning?

4. Why is it wrong to say that God tempts us? Where does our temptation come from?

5. What are some of the good gifts you have in your life? If every good gift comes from God, how should we respond to God and how should we treat our gifts?

NOTES

WEEK 2

For as the body apart from the spirit is dead, so also faith apart from works is dead.

JAMES 2:26

PRAYER

WRITE DOWN YOUR PRAYER REQUESTS
AND PRAISES FOR EACH DAY.

Prayer focus for this week:
Spend time praying for your country.

MONDAY

TUESDAY

WEDNESDAY

THURSDAY

FRIDAY

CHALLENGE
You can find this listed in our Monday blog post.

MONDAY
Scripture for Week 2

James 1:19-21

19 Know this, my beloved brothers: let every person be quick to hear, slow to speak, slow to anger; 20 for the anger of man does not produce the righteousness of God. 21 Therefore put away all filthiness and rampant wickedness and receive with meekness the implanted word, which is able to save your souls.

MONDAY

READ:
James 1:19-21

SOAP:
James 1:19-21

Scripture

WRITE
OUT THE
SCRIPTURE
PASSAGE
FOR THE
DAY.

Observations

WRITE
DOWN 1 OR 2
OBSERVATIONS
FROM THE
PASSAGE.

Applications

WRITE
DOWN 1 OR 2
APPLICATIONS
FROM THE
PASSAGE.

Pray

WRITE OUT
A PRAYER
OVER WHAT
YOU LEARNED
FROM TODAY'S
PASSAGE.

TUESDAY
Scripture for Week 2

James 1:22-27

22 But be doers of the word, and not hearers only, deceiving yourselves. 23 For if anyone is a hearer of the word and not a doer, he is like a man who looks intently at his natural face in a mirror. 24 For he looks at himself and goes away and at once forgets what he was like. 25 But the one who looks into the perfect law, the law of liberty, and perseveres, being no hearer who forgets but a doer who acts, he will be blessed in his doing.

26 If anyone thinks he is religious and does not bridle his tongue but deceives his heart, this person's religion is worthless. 27 Religion that is pure and undefiled before God the Father is this: to visit orphans and widows in their affliction, and to keep oneself unstained from the world.

TUESDAY

READ:
James 1:22-27

SOAP:
James 1:22-27

Scripture

WRITE
OUT THE
SCRIPTURE
PASSAGE
FOR THE
DAY.

Observations

WRITE
DOWN 1 OR 2
OBSERVATIONS
FROM THE
PASSAGE.

Applications

WRITE
DOWN 1 OR 2
APPLICATIONS
FROM THE
PASSAGE.

Pray

WRITE OUT
A PRAYER
OVER WHAT
YOU LEARNED
FROM TODAY'S
PASSAGE.

WEDNESDAY
Scripture for Week 2

James 2:1-7

1 My brothers, show no partiality as you hold the faith in
our Lord Jesus Christ, the Lord of glory. 2 For if a man
wearing a gold ring and fine clothing comes into your
assembly, and a poor man in shabby clothing also comes
in, 3 and if you pay attention to the one who wears the fine
clothing and say, "You sit here in a good place," while you
say to the poor man, "You stand over there," or, "Sit down
at my feet," 4 have you not then made distinctions among
yourselves and become judges with evil thoughts? 5 Listen,
my beloved brothers, has not God chosen those who
are poor in the world to be rich in faith and heirs of the
kingdom, which he has promised to those who love
him? 6 But you have dishonored the poor man. Are not
the rich the ones who oppress you, and the ones who drag
you into court? 7 Are they not the ones who blaspheme the
honorable name by which you were called?

WEDNESDAY

READ:
James 2:1-7

SOAP:
James 2:1-7

Scripture

WRITE
OUT THE
SCRIPTURE
PASSAGE
FOR THE
DAY.

Observations

WRITE
DOWN 1 OR 2
OBSERVATIONS
FROM THE
PASSAGE.

Applications

WRITE
DOWN 1 OR 2
APPLICATIONS
FROM THE
PASSAGE.

Pray

WRITE OUT
A PRAYER
OVER WHAT
YOU LEARNED
FROM TODAY'S
PASSAGE.

THURSDAY
Scripture for Week 2

James 2:8-13

8 If you really fulfill the royal law according to the Scripture, "You shall love your neighbor as yourself," you are doing well. 9 But if you show partiality, you are committing sin and are convicted by the law as transgressors. 10 For whoever keeps the whole law but fails in one point has become guilty of all of it. 11 For he who said, "Do not commit adultery," also said, "Do not murder." If you do not commit adultery but do murder, you have become a transgressor of the law. 12 So speak and so act as those who are to be judged under the law of liberty. 13 For judgment is without mercy to one who has shown no mercy. Mercy triumphs over judgment.

THURSDAY

READ:
James 2:8-13

SOAP:
James 2:8-9

Scripture

WRITE
OUT THE
SCRIPTURE
PASSAGE
FOR THE
DAY.

Observations

WRITE
DOWN 1 OR 2
OBSERVATIONS
FROM THE
PASSAGE.

Applications

WRITE
DOWN 1 OR 2
APPLICATIONS
FROM THE
PASSAGE.

Pray

WRITE OUT
A PRAYER
OVER WHAT
YOU LEARNED
FROM TODAY'S
PASSAGE.

FRIDAY
Scripture for Week 2

James 2:14-26

14 What good is it, my brothers, if someone says he has faith but does not have works? Can that faith save him? 15 If a brother or sister is poorly clothed and lacking in daily food, 16 and one of you says to them, "Go in peace, be warmed and filled," without giving them the things needed for the body, what good is that? 17 So also faith by itself, if it does not have works, is dead.

18 But someone will say, "You have faith and I have works." Show me your faith apart from your works, and I will show you my faith by my works. 19 You believe that God is one; you do well. Even the demons believe—and shudder! 20 Do you want to be shown, you foolish person, that faith apart from works is useless? 21 Was not Abraham our father justified by works when he offered up his son Isaac on the altar? 22 You see that faith was active along with his works, and faith was completed by his works; 23 and the Scripture was fulfilled that says, "Abraham believed God, and it was counted to him as righteousness"—and he was called a friend of God. 24 You see that a person is justified by works and not by faith alone. 25 And in the same way was not also Rahab the prostitute justified by works when she received the messengers and sent them out by another way? 26 For as the body apart from the spirit is dead, so also faith apart from works is dead.

FRIDAY

READ:
James 2:14-26

SOAP:
James 2:14-17

Scripture

WRITE
OUT THE
SCRIPTURE
PASSAGE
FOR THE
DAY.

Observations

WRITE
DOWN 1 OR 2
OBSERVATIONS
FROM THE
PASSAGE.

Applications

WRITE
DOWN 1 OR 2
APPLICATIONS
FROM THE
PASSAGE.

Pray

WRITE OUT
A PRAYER
OVER WHAT
YOU LEARNED
FROM TODAY'S
PASSAGE.

REFLECTION QUESTIONS

1. In what ways can we practice being slow to speak? How does anger go against the righteousness of God?

2. What is the importance of doing what God's Word tells us? When we only read and study but aren't "doers of the word", what does that show about ourselves? What is true religion?

3. What is the sin of partiality? Why is it bad? How do we fall into this sin?

4. Who has broken the law of God? How is it that if we break one part we are guilty of breaking all of it?

5. Throughout Scripture we are told that we are saved through faith, NOT by works (Eph. 2:8-9; Gal. 2:21; Rom. 9:16, 11:16). What does James mean when he says faith without works is dead?

NOTES

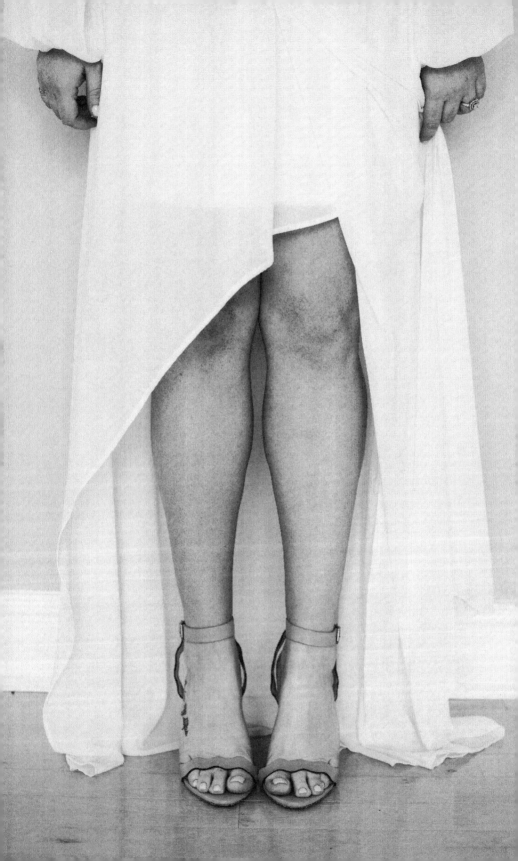

WEEK 3

The tongue also is a fire,
a world of evil among the parts
of the body. It corrupts the whole
body, sets the whole course of
one's life on fire, and is itself
set on fire by hell.

JAMES 3:6

PRAYER

Prayer focus for this week:
Spend time praying for your friends.

MONDAY

TUESDAY

WEDNESDAY

THURSDAY

FRIDAY

CHALLENGE

You can find this listed in our Monday blog post.

MONDAY
Scripture for Week 3

James 3:1-5

1 Not many of you should become teachers, my brothers, for you know that we who teach will be judged with greater strictness. 2 For we all stumble in many ways. And if anyone does not stumble in what he says, he is a perfect man, able also to bridle his whole body. 3 If we put bits into the mouths of horses so that they obey us, we guide their whole bodies as well. 4 Look at the ships also: though they are so large and are driven by strong winds, they are guided by a very small rudder wherever the will of the pilot directs. 5 So also the tongue is a small member, yet it boasts of great things.

How great a forest is set ablaze by such a small fire!

MONDAY

READ:
James 3:1-5

SOAP:
James 3:3-5

Scripture

WRITE
OUT THE
SCRIPTURE
PASSAGE
FOR THE
DAY.

Observations

WRITE
DOWN 1 OR 2
OBSERVATIONS
FROM THE
PASSAGE.

Applications

WRITE
DOWN 1 OR 2
APPLICATIONS
FROM THE
PASSAGE.

Pray

WRITE OUT
A PRAYER
OVER WHAT
YOU LEARNED
FROM TODAY'S
PASSAGE.

TUESDAY
Scripture for Week 3

James 3:6-12

6 And the tongue is a fire, a world of unrighteousness.
The tongue is set among our members, staining the whole
body, setting on fire the entire course of life, and set on
fire by hell. 7 For every kind of beast and bird, of reptile
and sea creature, can be tamed and has been tamed by
mankind, 8 but no human being can tame the tongue. It
is a restless evil, full of deadly poison. 9 With it we bless
our Lord and Father, and with it we curse people who are
made in the likeness of God. 10 From the same mouth come
blessing and cursing. My brothers, these things ought not
to be so.11 Does a spring pour forth from the same opening
both fresh and salt water?12 Can a fig tree, my brothers,
bear olives, or a grapevine produce figs? Neither can a salt
pond yield fresh water.

TUESDAY

READ:
James 3:6-12

SOAP:
James 3:8-10

Scripture

WRITE
OUT THE
SCRIPTURE
PASSAGE
FOR THE
DAY.

Observations

WRITE
DOWN 1 OR 2
OBSERVATIONS
FROM THE
PASSAGE.

Applications

WRITE
DOWN 1 OR 2
APPLICATIONS
FROM THE
PASSAGE.

Pray

WRITE OUT
A PRAYER
OVER WHAT
YOU LEARNED
FROM TODAY'S
PASSAGE.

WEDNESDAY
Scripture for Week 3

James 3:13-18

13 Who is wise and understanding among you? By his good conduct let him show his works in the meekness of wisdom. 14 But if you have bitter jealousy and selfish ambition in your hearts, do not boast and be false to the truth. 15 This is not the wisdom that comes down from above, but is earthly, unspiritual, demonic. 16 For where jealousy and selfish ambition exist, there will be disorder and every vile practice. 17 But the wisdom from above is first pure, then peaceable, gentle, open to reason, full of mercy and good fruits, impartial and sincere. 18 And a harvest of righteousness is sown in peace by those who make peace.

WEDNESDAY

READ:
James 3:13-18

SOAP:
James 3:17-18

Scripture

WRITE
OUT THE
SCRIPTURE
PASSAGE
FOR THE
DAY.

Observations

WRITE
DOWN 1 OR 2
OBSERVATIONS
FROM THE
PASSAGE.

Applications

WRITE
DOWN 1 OR 2
APPLICATIONS
FROM THE
PASSAGE.

Pray

WRITE OUT
A PRAYER
OVER WHAT
YOU LEARNED
FROM TODAY'S
PASSAGE.

THURSDAY
Scripture for Week 3

James 4:1-6

1 What causes quarrels and what causes fights among you? Is it not this, that your passions are at war within you? 2 You desire and do not have, so you murder. You covet and cannot obtain, so you fight and quarrel. You do not have, because you do not ask. 3 You ask and do not receive, because you ask wrongly, to spend it on your passions. 4 You adulterous people! Do you not know that friendship with the world is enmity with God? Therefore whoever wishes to be a friend of the world makes himself an enemy of God. 5 Or do you suppose it is to no purpose that the Scripture says, "He yearns jealously over the spirit that he has made to dwell in us"? 6 But he gives more grace. Therefore it says, "God opposes the proud but gives grace to the humble."

THURSDAY

READ:
James 4:1-6

SOAP:
James 4:4-6

Scripture

WRITE
OUT THE
SCRIPTURE
PASSAGE
FOR THE
DAY.

Observations

WRITE
DOWN 1 OR 2
OBSERVATIONS
FROM THE
PASSAGE.

Applications

WRITE
DOWN 1 OR 2
APPLICATIONS
FROM THE
PASSAGE.

Pray

WRITE OUT
A PRAYER
OVER WHAT
YOU LEARNED
FROM TODAY'S
PASSAGE.

FRIDAY
Scripture for Week 3

James 4:7-12

7 Submit yourselves therefore to God. Resist the devil, and
he will flee from you. 8 Draw near to God, and he will draw
near to you. Cleanse your hands, you sinners, and purify
your hearts, you double-minded. 9 Be wretched and mourn
and weep. Let your laughter be turned to mourning and
your joy to gloom. 10 Humble yourselves before the Lord,
and he will exalt you.

11 Do not speak evil against one another, brothers. The one
who speaks against a brother or judges his brother, speaks
evil against the law and judges the law. But if you judge the
law, you are not a doer of the law but a judge. 12 There is
only one lawgiver and judge, he who is able to save and to
destroy. But who are you to judge your neighbor?

FRIDAY

READ:
James 4:7-12

SOAP:
James 4:7-8

Scripture

WRITE
OUT THE
SCRIPTURE
PASSAGE
FOR THE
DAY.

Observations

WRITE
DOWN 1 OR 2
OBSERVATIONS
FROM THE
PASSAGE.

Applications

WRITE
DOWN 1 OR 2
APPLICATIONS
FROM THE
PASSAGE.

Pray

WRITE OUT
A PRAYER
OVER WHAT
YOU LEARNED
FROM TODAY'S
PASSAGE.

REFLECTION QUESTIONS

1. Why is it so hard to control the tongue?

2. What is the danger of not controlling our tongue?

3. What is the difference between heavenly wisdom and earthly wisdom? How do you know which one you have?

4. How is friendship with the world adultery towards God? How do we stay faithful?

5. Are we allowed to judge others? Why or why not?

NOTES

WEEK 4

You also, be patient.
Establish your hearts,
for the coming of the
Lord is at hand.

JAMES 5:8

PRAYER

Prayer focus for this week:
Spend time praying for your church.

MONDAY

TUESDAY

WEDNESDAY

THURSDAY

FRIDAY

CHALLENGE

You can find this listed in our Monday blog post.

MONDAY
Scripture for Week 4

James 4:13-17

13 Come now, you who say, "Today or tomorrow we will go into such and such a town and spend a year there and trade and make a profit"— 14 yet you do not know what tomorrow will bring. What is your life? For you are a mist that appears for a little time and then vanishes. 15 Instead you ought to say, "If the Lord wills, we will live and do this or that." 16 As it is, you boast in your arrogance. All such boasting is evil. 17 So whoever knows the right thing to do and fails to do it, for him it is sin.

MONDAY

READ:
James 4:13-17

SOAP:
James 4:13-17

Scripture

WRITE
OUT THE
SCRIPTURE
PASSAGE
FOR THE
DAY.

Observations

WRITE
DOWN 1 OR 2
OBSERVATIONS
FROM THE
PASSAGE.

Applications

WRITE
DOWN 1 OR 2
APPLICATIONS
FROM THE
PASSAGE.

Pray

WRITE OUT
A PRAYER
OVER WHAT
YOU LEARNED
FROM TODAY'S
PASSAGE.

TUESDAY
Scripture for Week 4

James 5:1-6

1 Come now, you rich, weep and howl for the miseries that are coming upon you. 2 Your riches have rotted and your garments are moth-eaten. 3 Your gold and silver have corroded, and their corrosion will be evidence against you and will eat your flesh like fire. You have laid up treasure in the last days. 4 Behold, the wages of the laborers who mowed your fields, which you kept back by fraud, are crying out against you, and the cries of the harvesters have reached the ears of the Lord of hosts. 5 You have lived on the earth in luxury and in self-indulgence. You have fattened your hearts in a day of slaughter. 6 You have condemned and murdered the righteous person. He does not resist you.

TUESDAY

READ:
James 5:1-6

SOAP:
James 5:1-3

Scripture

WRITE
OUT THE
SCRIPTURE
PASSAGE
FOR THE
DAY.

Observations

WRITE
DOWN 1 OR 2
OBSERVATIONS
FROM THE
PASSAGE.

Applications

WRITE
DOWN 1 OR 2
APPLICATIONS
FROM THE
PASSAGE.

Pray

WRITE OUT
A PRAYER
OVER WHAT
YOU LEARNED
FROM TODAY'S
PASSAGE.

WEDNESDAY

Scripture for Week 4

James 5:7-12

7 Be patient, therefore, brothers, until the coming of the
Lord. See how the farmer waits for the precious fruit of
the earth, being patient about it, until it receives the early
and the late rains. 8 You also, be patient. Establish your
hearts, for the coming of the Lord is at hand. 9 Do not
grumble against one another, brothers, so that you may not
be judged; behold, the Judge is standing at the door. 10 As
an example of suffering and patience, brothers, take the
prophets who spoke in the name of the Lord. 11 Behold,
we consider those blessed who remained steadfast. You have
heard of the steadfastness of Job, and you have seen the
purpose of the Lord, how the Lord is compassionate and
merciful.

12 But above all, my brothers, do not swear, either by
heaven or by earth or by any other oath, but let your "yes"
be yes and your "no" be no, so that you may not fall under
condemnation.

WEDNESDAY

READ:
James 5:7-12

SOAP:
James 5:7-8

Scripture

WRITE
OUT THE
SCRIPTURE
PASSAGE
FOR THE
DAY.

Observations

WRITE
DOWN 1 OR 2
OBSERVATIONS
FROM THE
PASSAGE.

Applications

WRITE
DOWN 1 OR 2
APPLICATIONS
FROM THE
PASSAGE.

Pray

WRITE OUT
A PRAYER
OVER WHAT
YOU LEARNED
FROM TODAY'S
PASSAGE.

THURSDAY
Scripture for Week 4

James 5:13-18

13 Is anyone among you suffering? Let him pray. Is anyone cheerful? Let him sing praise. 14 Is anyone among you sick? Let him call for the elders of the church, and let them pray over him, anointing him with oil in the name of the Lord. 15 And the prayer of faith will save the one who is sick, and the Lord will raise him up. And if he has committed sins, he will be forgiven. 16 Therefore, confess your sins to one another and pray for one another, that you may be healed. The prayer of a righteous person has great power as it is working. 17 Elijah was a man with a nature like ours, and he prayed fervently that it might not rain, and for three years and six months it did not rain on the earth. 18 Then he prayed again, and heaven gave rain, and the earth bore its fruit.

THURSDAY

READ:
James 5:13-18

SOAP:
James 5:13-16

Scripture

WRITE
OUT THE
SCRIPTURE
PASSAGE
FOR THE
DAY.

Observations

WRITE
DOWN 1 OR 2
OBSERVATIONS
FROM THE
PASSAGE.

Applications

WRITE
DOWN 1 OR 2
APPLICATIONS
FROM THE
PASSAGE.

Pray

WRITE OUT
A PRAYER
OVER WHAT
YOU LEARNED
FROM TODAY'S
PASSAGE.

FRIDAY
Scripture for Week 4

James 5:19-20

19 My brothers, if anyone among you wanders from the truth and someone brings him back, 20 let him know that whoever brings back a sinner from his wandering will save his soul from death and will cover a multitude of sins.

FRIDAY

READ:
James 5:19-20

SOAP:
James 5:19-20

Scripture

WRITE
OUT THE
SCRIPTURE
PASSAGE
FOR THE
DAY.

Observations

WRITE
DOWN 1 OR 2
OBSERVATIONS
FROM THE
PASSAGE.

Applications

WRITE
DOWN 1 OR 2
APPLICATIONS
FROM THE
PASSAGE.

Pray

WRITE OUT
A PRAYER
OVER WHAT
YOU LEARNED
FROM TODAY'S
PASSAGE.

REFLECTION QUESTIONS

1. How should we handle plans we make for the future? What kind of attitude should we have?

2. Why does James give such a harsh warning to the rich (verses 1-6)?

3. Why is patience so important during times of suffering? How can it help us?

4. How powerful is prayer? Why do we not pray as often or as earnestly as we should?

5. What are some practical ways of handling someone who has "wandered from the truth"?

NOTES

KNOW THESE TRUTHS
from God's Word

God loves you.

Even when you're feeling unworthy and like the world is stacked against you, God loves you - yes, you - and He has created you for great purpose.

God's Word says, "God so loved the world that He gave His one and only Son, Jesus, that whoever believes in Him shall not perish, but have eternal life" (John 3:16).

Our sin separates us from God.

We are all sinners by nature and by choice, and because of this we are separated from God, who is holy.

God's Word says, "All have sinned and fall short of the glory of God" (Romans 3:23).

Jesus died so that you might have life.

The consequence of sin is death, but your story doesn't have to end there! God's free gift of salvation is available to us because Jesus took the penalty for our sin when He died on the cross.

God's Word says, "For the wages of sin is death, but the free gift of God is eternal life in Christ Jesus our Lord" (Romans 6:23); "God demonstrates His own love toward us, in that while we were yet sinners, Christ died for us" (Romans 5:8).

Jesus lives!

Death could not hold Him, and three days after His body was placed in the tomb Jesus rose again, defeating sin and death forever! He lives today in heaven and is preparing a place in eternity for all who believe in Him.

God's Word says, "In my Father's house are many rooms. If it were not so, would I have told you that I go to prepare a place for you? And if I go and prepare a place for you, I will come again and will take you to myself, that where I am you may be also" (John 14:2-3).

Yes, you can KNOW that you are forgiven.
Accept Jesus as the only way to salvation...

Accepting Jesus as your Savior is not about what you can do, but rather about having faith in what Jesus has already done. It takes recognizing that you are a sinner, believing that Jesus died for your sins, and asking for forgiveness by placing your full trust in Jesus's work on the cross on your behalf.

God's Word says, "If you confess with your mouth that Jesus is Lord and believe in your heart that God raised him from the dead, you will be saved. For with the heart one believes and is justified, and with the mouth one confesses and is saved" (Romans 10:9-10).

Practically, what does that look like?
With a sincere heart, you can pray a simple prayer like this:

God,
I know that I am a sinner.
I don't want to live another day without embracing
the love and forgiveness that You have for me.
I ask for Your forgiveness.
I believe that You died for my sins and rose from the dead.
I surrender all that I am and ask You to be Lord of my life.
Help me to turn from my sin and follow You.
Teach me what it means to walk in freedom as I live under Your grace,
and help me to grow in Your ways as I seek to know You more.
Amen.

If you just prayed this prayer (or something similar in your own words), would you email us at info@lovegodgreatly.com?

We'd love to help get you started on this exciting journey as a child of God!

WELCOME FRIEND

We're so glad you're here

Love God Greatly exists to inspire, encourage, and equip women all over the world to make God's Word a priority in their lives.

INSPIRE
women to make God's Word a priority in their daily lives through our Bible study resources.

ENCOURAGE
women in their daily walks with God through online community and personal accountability.

EQUIP
women to grow in their faith, so that they can effectively reach others for Christ.

Love God Greatly consists of a beautiful community of women who use a variety of technology platforms to keep each other accountable in God's Word.

We start with a simple Bible reading plan, but it doesn't stop there.

Some gather in homes and churches locally, while others connect online with women across the globe. Whatever the method, we lovingly lock arms and unite for this purpose...to Love God Greatly with our lives.

At Love God Greatly, you'll find real, authentic women. Women who are imperfect, yet forgiven. Women who desire less of us, and a whole lot more of Jesus. Women who long to know God through his Word, because we know that Truth transforms and sets us free. Women who are better together, saturated in God's Word and in community with one another.

Love God Greatly is a 501 (C) (3) non-profit organization. Funding for Love God Greatly comes through donations and proceeds from our online Bible study journals and books. LGG is committed to providing quality Bible study materials and believes finances should never get in the way of a woman being able to participate in one of our studies. All journals and translated journals are available to download for free from LoveGodGreatly.com for those who cannot afford to purchase them. Our journals and books are also available for sale on Amazon. Search for "Love God Greatly" to see all of our Bible study journals and books. 100% of proceeds go directly back into supporting Love God Greatly and helping us inspire, encourage and equip women all over the world with God's Word.

THANK YOU for partnering with us!

WHAT WE OFFER:

18 + Translations | Bible Reading Plans | Online Bible Study
Love God Greatly App | 80 + Countries Served
Bible Study Journals & Books | Community Groups

EACH LGG STUDY INCLUDES:

Three Devotional Corresponding Blog Posts
Memory Verses | Weekly Challenge | Weekly Reading Plan
Reflection Questions And More!

OTHER LOVE GOD GREATLY STUDIES INCLUDE:

David | Ecclesiastes | Growing Through Prayer | Names Of God
Galatians | Psalm 119 | 1st & 2nd Peter | Made For Community | Esther
The Road To Christmas | The Source Of Gratitude | You Are Loved

Visit us online at
LOVEGODGREATLY.COM